SHOUT ™

A LOUD AND LIVELY BOOK SHOWCASING THE TALENTS, THOUGHTS, IDEAS AND VOICES OF KIDS WHO ARE DIFFERENTLY "ABLE."

Pat Loewi

SHOUT. A Loud and Lively Book Showcasing the Talents, Thoughts, Ideas and Voices of Kids Who Are Differently "Able" by Pat Loewi

Books may be purchased in quantity and/or special sales by contacting the publisher, SHOUT Inc.
PO Box 200755
Denver, Colorado 80220
or
By faxing 303-322-7992
or
By emailing shouteffect@gmail.com
or
Online at www.shouteffect.org

SHOUT. A Loud and Lively Book Showcasing the Talents, Thoughts, Ideas and Voices of Kids Who Are Differently "Able."

Library of Congress Catalog Card No. 2015914974

ISBN: 978-1-4951-7239-7

Category Education
First Edition Volume 001

Book Design by Cheryl Patrick
Printed in the United States of America

All net profits will be donated to qualifying participating non-profit organizations.

THIS BOOK IS DEDICATED
TO KIM AND SAMMY, WHO TAUGHT
ME ALL ABOUT UNCONDITIONAL LOVE, AND
TO MY PRECIOUS GRANDDAUGHTERS
FINLEY, SELBY AND OLIVE.

"THERE IS A SUPERHERO INSIDE OF US.
WE JUST NEED THE COURAGE TO
PUT ON THE CAPE."

-unknown

TABLE OF CONTENTS

A sincere thank you to the following organizations for making this book possible and a detailed description of each: Muscular Dystrophy Association, Easter Seals of Colorado, Special Olympics Colorado, Colorado Center for the Blind, Children's Hospital of Colorado, 2Hearts Congenital Heart Disease Program, Global Down Syndrome Foundation, MDA Art Collection, VSA Colorado/Access Gallery, and Roundup River Ranch.

SHOUT

it from the rooftops!
Our beautiful girl is here.

Samantha came to us when she was five days old after my husband Andy and I had experienced five years of gut-wrenching infertility treatments and two heart-breaking failed adoptions. We were thrilled beyond words with our beautiful blue-eyed baby. Little did we know that over the years, Sammy would come to be our biggest teacher in life lessons. She was a wise soul that would show us unbelievable courage and tenacity. And, she had a gentle heart with a love of rock and roll who would turn every event into pure joy and teach us the ultimate lessons of how to live life out loud.

In spite of battling muscular dystrophy, Sammy made the absolute most of every moment until she died unexpectedly of pulmonary edema at age 22. Her death was devastating. I not only lost a daughter, but also a mentor whose never-give-up attitude inspired me daily. I wanted to shout out in pain, shout at someone in anger, shout that I couldn't take life without her. But that is certainly not what Sammy would have wanted. She would have wanted me to make noise by making a meaningful difference in the world. So I have mustered up my own voice and the voice of so many others.

SHOUT **is a celebration of the far-reaching "voice" Sammy had during her life.** She spoke up often and loudly for others. She raised her voice for awareness and fairness, for answers and hope. She, like many other young people with physical, intellectual and medical challenges, simply wanted the world to look past what made them "different" and listen—really listen—to who they were and what they had to offer.

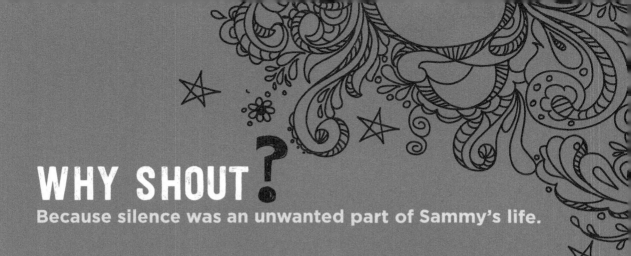

WHY SHOUT?

Because silence was an unwanted part of Sammy's life.

People who passed Sammy in her wheelchair on the street would often either stare quietly or look right past her. This was so frustrating for a girl who was bursting with things to talk about! But, that's how it often is for kids with disabilities. They are either overlooked or objects of fascination.

If anyone took the time to break the silence, look past the wheelchair and get to know Sammy, here's what they'd find out about the lovely (and loud) woman they would meet:

Sammy was diagnosed with muscular dystrophy when she was 18 months old. By age two, her ferocious determination had already begun to appear. Even though she'd totter around on unstable legs, her whole demeanor screamed, "I don't need your help! I can do it myself!"—and often, she could.

By age nine, Sammy was unable to walk more than five or six steps without assistance, so we got her a bright blue scooter to help her get between classes at school. Her teacher asked her to talk with the class about her disability and I stood in the back of the classroom as Sammy confidently explained to 30 able-bodied classmates, "I have congenital muscular dystrophy and it makes my muscles weak so that's why I need a scooter. It doesn't affect anything else I do and it isn't contagious."

The next year, her fourth-grade teachers announced that the class could pick a community project in which to get involved. Because I was working at Special Olympics of Colorado at the time, Sammy suggested that her class create a Special Olympics Day—and they did. It was a day in which the kids at her school were paired with kids from nearby special education classes. The goal was to help kids learn to celebrate their similarities instead of focusing on their differences. That single day at Sammy's school has since evolved into a year-long buddy program named in her honor and still taking place years later.

(It is a laugh-out-loud, play-out-loud, ignore-differences day program that can be replicated by schools of any size. To help make that happen, we've included a detailed description of the Graland Sammy Loewi Unified Games in the Appendix.)

By the time she was 12, Sammy had become fascinated with professions she knew would be impossible for her. "Mom," she'd say, "I want to be a break dancer." Or, "I want to be a policewoman and carry a gun." Or, "I want to be a test pilot in the Air Force." All this from a child who couldn't get out of bed by herself. She literally was dreaming out loud.

Although Sammy needed help getting dressed, and with toileting, hair brushing and bathing, there was so much she *could* do and she focused her energies there. She played the piano for 11 years, as well as the soprano saxophone and base guitar.

She swam three times a week from the time she was two, eventually entering the National Disability Swimming Competition, where she set national records in the backstroke and the front crawl—even though her arms and legs were bent due to permanent muscle shortening.

She was an artist who painted aspen trees in the first grade, portraits of fellow students in the ninth grade, and seriously pursued both expressive art and darkroom photography in college.

Because Sammy was so desperate to gain some independence, she—with the help of her older sister Kim—spent eight months and hundreds of hours learning to drive a wheelchair-accessible van outfitted with hand controls.

She was also a passionate activist on behalf of all people with disabilities. She spent three years as a spokesperson for the Colorado Muscular Dystrophy Association. She offered to prepare a video for airline executives to sensitize them to the challenges of traveling in a wheelchair. (Her wheelchair had been damaged countless times by careless baggage handlers). She wrote a letter to the U.S. Department of Veterans Affairs seeking volunteer opportunities to help soldiers returning from war in wheelchairs.

When she died, Sammy was in the middle of creating a company to benefit physically challenged people. Her company—which she called Unraveled—was being created to help design, manufacture and sell attractive and practical clothing for people in wheelchairs.

OF COURSE THE TEENAGE YEARS BECAME EVEN LOUDER. BUT SAMMY HAD A GOOD REASON FOR IT.

Because the world often chose to look straight through Sammy and her chair, as a teenager she found fun (and sometimes flamboyant!) ways to say, "Hey, I'm here, pay attention!" She streaked her hair pink. She saved up her allowance and talked her after-school sitter into taking her to get her earlobes stretched (much to my dismay). She dyed her hair bright red, then orange with dark streaks, then black again with blond streaks. She pierced the top of her ears with thin two-inch silver rods. To cap it off, one day I noticed something tattooed in two-inch black hieroglyphics along the inside of her left arm.

"Oh Sammy," I said, "What have you done?"

"Mom, it says *FEARLESS.*"

"Sammy, when will it all stop?" I asked her. "When will you stop punishing your body?"

She paused and then very thoughtfully explained, "Mom, I'm tired of being invisible. Every time someone walks toward me in my wheelchair they either look away like they are embarrassed or act as if they are looking right through me—like I don't exist."

Suddenly, her actions and appearance made sense to me. Here was a kid trying to get her independence from us, which was nearly impossible because of her physical dependence, but also a young woman struggling to be noticed for more than her disability.

Sammy took me noisily and happily to places I might never have gone in life.

Throughout her too-short life, Sammy needed my assistance to do most everything. I helped her to literally get from place to place, but she took me places I never would have gone without her. She taught me how to be fearless and strong, how to push forward without complaint, how to push back when treated unfairly and what it means to be truly authentic. I miss her every second of every day. The loss is enormous. The hole she left is impossible to fill.

NOW, IT'S TIME TO USE SAMMY'S INSPIRATION TO SHOUT ABOUT ALL THE OTHER AMAZING KIDS AND YOUNG ADULTS OUT THERE WHO ARE MAKING THEIR OWN MAGIC IN THE WORLD.

SHOUT was created to help readers understand that all kids with physical, intellectual and medical challenges are far more than their disability. They are kids with ambition, insight, courage, wisdom, passion, pizzazz, tenacity, joy and humor.

The other motivation behind this book (besides the fact that I can literally hear Sammy egging me on!) is that I want to help readers understand and appreciate that people with disabilities are sensitive human beings with feelings. In high school, Sammy was often ignored or excluded by other students and she spent most of her time alone. This is typical, as kids with disabilities are often overlooked by their classmates. Worse yet, children with disabilities are *two to three times more likely* than other students to be bullied for being different *(see the special Bullying Section in the Appendix).*

But once you get to know these kids you realize they are not so different after all. They want to be asked their opinion. They want to show off their talents. They want to engage and be heard. The pages in this book are a way of showing off their voices and their artwork, their thoughts and their talents.

If you like what you see, if it opens up your eyes to what these kids are really like, if it changes your perceptions—***Shout*** about it! This is a story the world needs to hear.

Sincerely,

Pat Loewi

WE ALL HAVE WISHES THAT WE KEEP QUIETLY INSIDE. BUT WHAT IF WE LET THEM OUT? WHAT IF BY SAYING THEM, WE COULD MAKE THEM COME TRUE?

I WISH

I WISH PEOPLE WOULDN'T TELL ME THAT I AM LYING ABOUT BEING SICK JUST TO GET OUT OF SCHOOL.

– **Jodi**, 12, Heart Disease

Artwork by Collaborative Group, VSA Colorado/Access Gallery

Artwork by Jackie, 18, Autism

I wish people would be happy all the time. – Sydney, 8, Diabetes

I wish people wouldn't make fun of me because I have diabetes.

– Bren, 12, Diabetes

Artwork by Sunia, 18, Autism

I WISH PEOPLE WOULD STOP AND THINK ABOUT WHAT THEY SAY AND DO TO PEOPLE WITH DISABILITIES AND MEDICAL CONDITIONS— LIKE NOT PUSHING A WHEELCHAIR TOO FAST, OR MAKING FUN OF PEOPLE, OR TRIPPING A BLIND PERSON, OR GIVING CHOCOLATE TO SOMEONE WHO IS ALLERGIC.

– Sven, 13, Cyclic Vomiting

I WISH PEOPLE WOULD TRY TO COMPREHEND AND UNDERSTAND MY SITUATION A LITTLE MORE SOMETIMES.

– Todd, 16, Diabetes

Artwork by Trevor, 16, Spinal Muscular Atrophy

Artwork by Jared, 17, Autism

I wish people would treat me like a normal kid. Often, when I walk somewhere, kids look at me strange.

– Joseph, 12, Kidney Disease

I WISH PEOPLE WOULD BE ABLE to RELATE to ME AND MY ILLNESS, AND HAVE MORE PATIENCE WITH ME ABOUT It. I ALSO WISH I COULD NOT BE A DIABETIC — DUH! - Angela, 17, Diabetes

Artwork by Collaborative Group, VSA Colorado/Access Gallery

I WISH THAT I COULD RIDE A BIKE.

– Carrie, 9, Seizure Disorder

Artwork by David, 10, Duchenne Muscular Dystrophy

I WISH THAT IN THE FUTURE EVERYONE WHO WANTS TO WILL BE ABLE TO WALK.

– Bjorn, 10, Muscular Dystrophy

Artwork by Mallory, 13, Limb-Girdle Muscular Dystrophy

I'd like to see the whole world become more accessible. – Evan, 15, Muscular Dystrophy

EVERYBODY HAS CHALLENGES. SOME ARE OBVIOUS. SOME ARE HARD TO SEE UNLESS YOU REALLY GET TO KNOW A PERSON. LET'S CHALLENGE OURSELVES TO BE MORE EMPATHIC ABOUT THE TOUGH ROADS OTHERS ARE TRAVELING.

LIFE'S A CHALLENGE

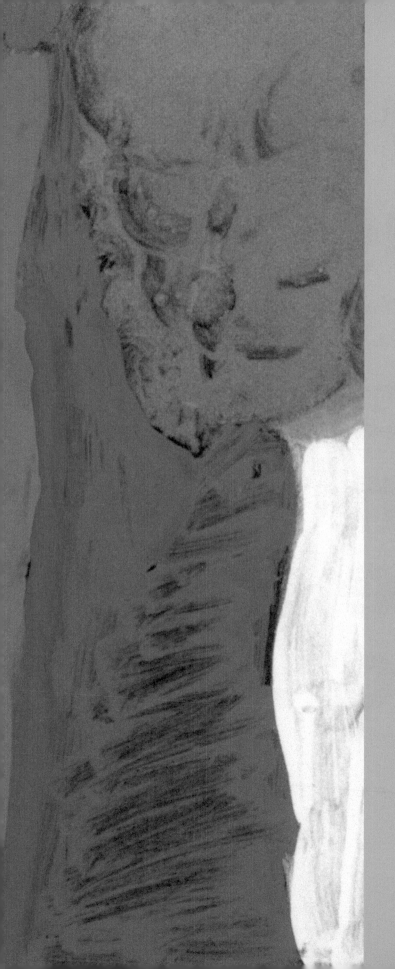

IT'S TOUGH FOR ME TO FORM FRIENDSHIPS. WHEN I'M INVITED TO SOMEONE'S HOUSE, I'M AFRAID TO ASK IF THEY HAVE STAIRS.

– John, 16, Muscular Dystrophy

Artwork by Chad, 9,
Duchenne Muscular
Dystrophy

It's hard going to school because it isn't fun to be made fun of.

– Debbie, 16, Intellectual Challenge

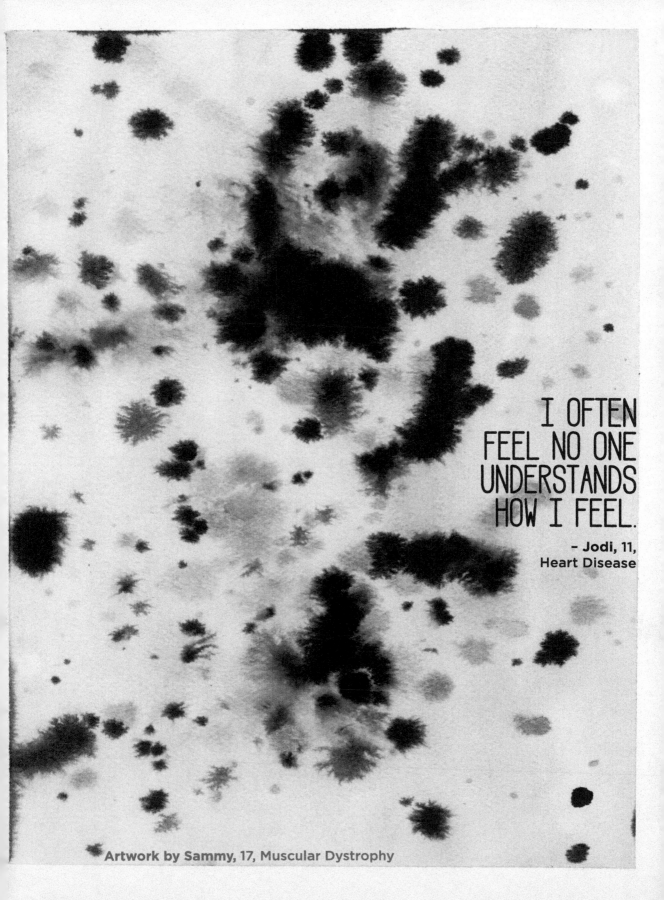

I OFTEN
FEEL NO ONE
UNDERSTANDS
HOW I FEEL.

— **Jodi, 11,**
Heart Disease

Artwork by Sammy, 17, Muscular Dystrophy

Artwork by Jackie, 18, Autism

I have to be really, really careful with practically everything I do.
It's hard sometimes when I want to do something cool, like climbing
a mountain. My ankles start to bleed and it's frustrating.

— **Jordan,** 10, Hemophilia

MY CEREBRAL PALSY CAUSES MY BRAIN AND MUSCLES TO BE UNCONNECTED—AND I'M TIGHT ALL THE TIME.

Artwork by Allie, 18, Autism

– Alana, 16, Cerebral Palsy

Most of the time, I feel physically, emotionally and mentally exhausted.

– Alan, 16, Alport Syndrome

**Artwork by Amie, 18,
Learning Disability**

Artwork by A.J, 17, Autism

It's kind of hard because I need infusions every other day and I have to take lots of breaks because I get tired easily. I don't get to do fun things like football.

– Matt, 9, Severe Hemophilia

The hardest part about having a heart problem is pain.

sometimes it just hurts.

— Kenneth, 11, Congenital Heart Disease

I PREFER TO KEEP
MY HEMO **A SECRET.**

I'M AFRAID ONCE PEOPLE
KNOW THEY WILL TREAT
ME DIFFERENTLY.

– Kendall, 12, Hemophilia

Artwork by Sammy, 18, Muscular Dystrophy

I HAVE NON-STOP NOSEBLEEDS AND AN INSULIN PUMP IN MY SIDE.

– Corrine, 11,
Blood Clotting Disorder
and Type 1 Diabetes

Artwork by Crystal, 15, Mitochondrial Myopathy

WISDOM IS TOUGH. YOU HAVE TO WORK FOR IT. GET THROUGH
SOME HARD DAYS. LAY AWAKE THROUGH SOME LONG NIGHTS.
BUT WHEN YOU GAIN WISDOM, NO ONE CAN
EVER TAKE IT AWAY FROM YOU. AND THAT'S POWERFUL.

HARD-EARNED WISDOM

When people make positive statements, they get stronger.

When they make negative statements, they get weaker.
- Ryan, 12, Muscular Dystrophy

Artwork by Sammy, 16, Muscular Dystrophy

EVERY MORNING I WAKE UP AND THINK 'WHAT CAN I DO TO MAKE MY LIFE COUNT?'

– Shawn, 15, Duchenne Muscular Dystrophy

Artwork by Aubrey, 11, Friedreich's Ataxia

People with disabilities
know it's not okay to engage
in offensive behavior.

– Peter, 17, Stroke

**Artwork by Collaborative Group,
VSA Colorado/Access Gallery**

MY FRIENDS ACT LIKE EVERY DAY IS JUST LIKE THE ONE BEFORE. FOR ME, EVERY DAY IS A NEW START.

– Evan, 15, Duchenne Muscular Dystrophy

Artwork by Louis, 18, Intellectually Challenged

I believe that God gives us struggles so we can connect with others on a deeper level.

– **Sarah,** 16, Arthrogryposis Multiplex Congenita

Artwork by Jose Carballo, 17,
Duchenne Muscular Dystrophy

I don't care what people look like.
We're all the same inside.

– Zak, 17, Duchenne Muscular Dystrophy

Artwork by Christina, 13, Friedreich's Ataxia

YOU KNOW SOMEONE IS A GREAT PERSON BY HOW THEY TREAT OTHERS.

– Hannah, 19, Intellectual Disability

Artwork by Elsha, 15, Spinal Muscular Atrophy

I MAY HAVE PHYSICAL CHALLENGES THAT ARE ANNOYING AND FRUSTRATING, BUT IN REALITY I KNOW WE ARE ALL THE SAME: HUMAN.

– Ethan, 19, Duchenne Muscular Dystrophy

BULLIES HURT PEOPLE SO DEEPLY THE SCARS CAN'T EVEN BE SEEN.
BUT THEY'RE THERE. SOMETIMES FOREVER. THAT'S WHY IT'S
NEVER, EVER, EVER, EVER, EVER OK TO BE MEAN TO SOMEONE.

ON BULLYING

*

NEVER, EVER, EVER, EVER, EVER, EVER, EVER, EVER, EVER, EVER, EVER, EVER, EVER, EVER,

I wish people would
judging and

stop bullying other people.

– Alicia, 16, Obesity

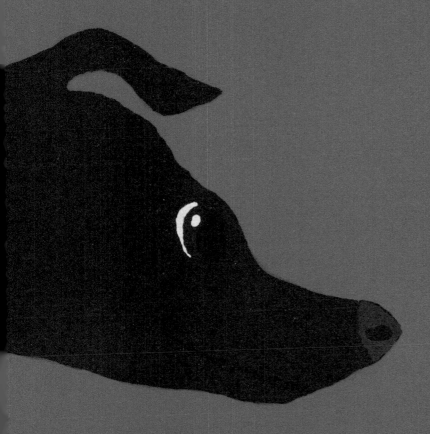

Artwork by Allie, 18, Autism

I WAS
BULLIED
IN 6TH
GRADE.
A GIRL
CALLED
ME
'STUPID'
AND
ANOTHER
GIRL
FOLLOWED
ME HOME
FROM
SCHOOL
ONE DAY
AND It
SCARED
ME.

– Amy, 14,
Intellectual
Disability

Artwork by Nicole, 17, Developmental Disability

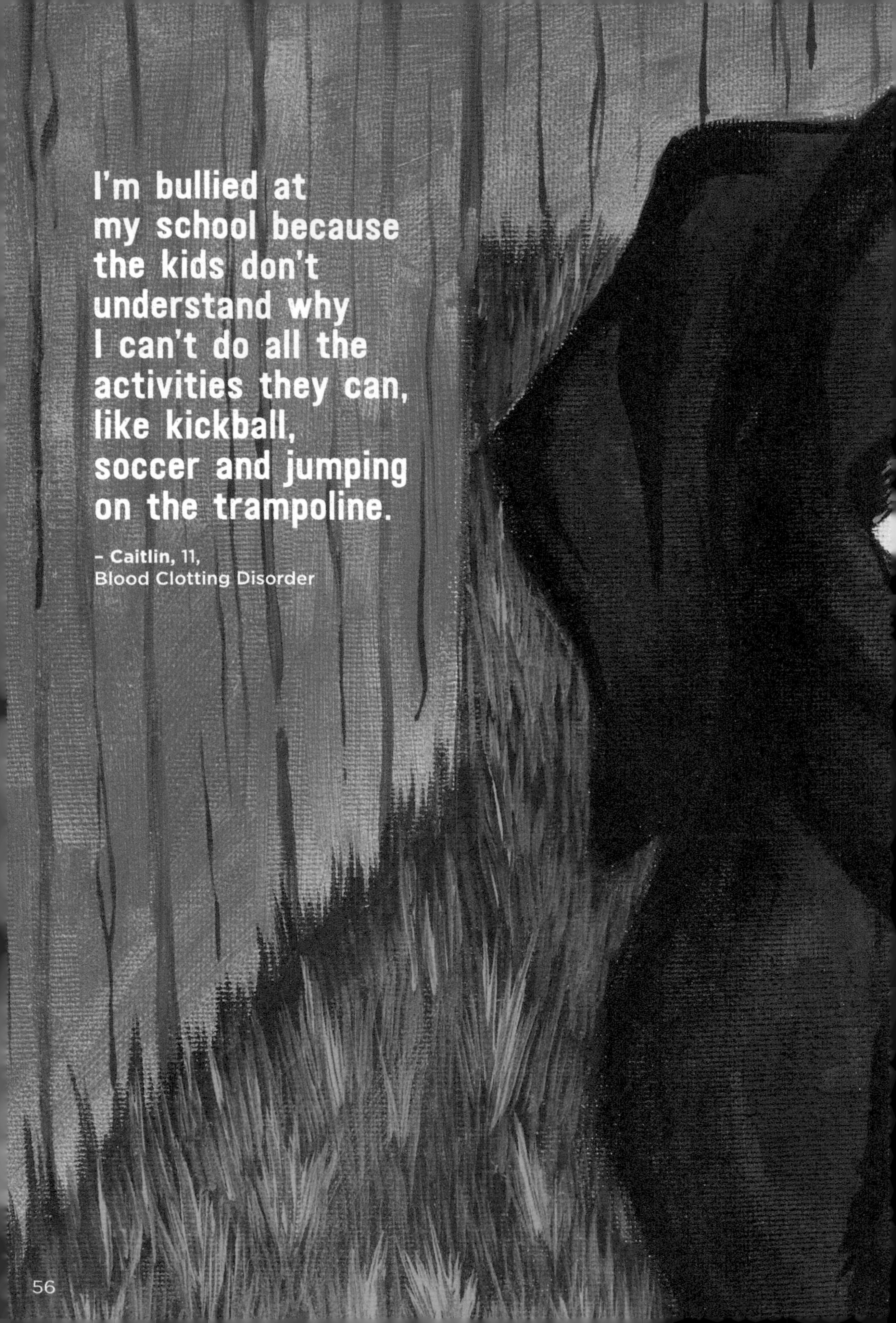

I'm bullied at
my school because
the kids don't
understand why
I can't do all the
activities they can,
like kickball,
soccer and jumping
on the trampoline.

– Caitlin, 11,
Blood Clotting Disorder

Artwork by
Amie, 18,
Learning Disability

THE BULLIES, a poem

This journey started with the bullies

They were a group of three girls walking down the crowded hallway looking stylish,

fashionable, better

Better than who?

Me, my other peers? No, they were just, the bullies

Taunting me daily, they didn't care

Care for my emotions, my thoughts, and my life

My life was different, I was different

Different how?

Different hair, different color, different thinking

I was me and they were them

Teachers, friends, not knowing what I was going through

And attack!

They would come for me manipulating, strategizing, brainstorming What's next?

Like a bird away from its flock

Confused, cautious, like a yellow light on a busy, rush hour street

Scarce shootings, multiple suicides, by kids my age all over the state, the world

They had just had, enough!

– Cassandra, 16, Congenital Heart Disease

THE THINGS WE ARE DEALING WITH TODAY MAY SLOW US DOWN, OR CHANGE OUR COURSE. BUT THEY DON'T STOP US FROM PLANNING ALL OF OUR TOMORROWS. BECAUSE EVERY DAY IS A BRAND NEW START.

WHEN I GROW UP

AFTER HIGH SCHOOL I WANT TO BE IN THE NAVY. I LIKE ADVENTURE AND USING WEAPONS AND... I WANT TO BE SOMEONE'S HERO.

– Tasha, 14, Muscular Dystrophy

I'D LIKE TO BE AN INVENTOR SO THAT I CAN INVENT BETTER LEGS TO HELP PEOPLE WHO CAN'T WALK.

– Bjorn, 10, Muscular Dystrophy

Artwork by Andrew, 9, Becker Muscular Dystrophy

Artwork by Collaborative Group, VSA Gallery

I want to help people with disabilities get out of nursing homes and live independently. And, I will continue to fight for productive immigrants to get amnesty.

– Mario, 18,
Duchenne Muscular Dystrophy

I'm a good golfer. It's my dream to be the first special needs golfer to join the Tour.

– Vincent, 19, Intellectual Disability

I want to be a professional athlete.
Not on a disabled team, but a regular team.

– Bjorn, 10, Muscular Dystrophy

I want to go to college for massage therapy, start a family, live life, and hope there will be a cure for me someday.

– Candace, 17, Diabetes

**Artwork by Craig, 17,
Spinal Muscular Atrophy**

I WANT TO BE AN AUTHOR WHEN I GROW UP AND HAVE ALREADY WRITTEN A BOOK ABOUT A GIRL WHO USES MIND CONTROL TO MOVE THINGS.

– Katrina, 14, Blind

Artwork by Sammy, 15, Muscular Dystrophy

I want to be a professional photographer and be happy.

– Alicia, 16, Acute Liver Failure and Obesity

WHEN YOU LOOK IN THE MIRROR AND THE PERSON LOOKING BACK MAKES YOU SMILE, THERE IS NO GREATER FEELING. AFTER ALL, THAT'S THE PERSON YOU HAVE TO LIVE WITH EVERY DAY FOR YOUR WHOLE LIFE.

FEELING PROUD

Strengths I've gained
from being blind?

1

I don't judge people based
on what they look like.

2

I can read in the dark.

3

When the power goes out in
our house I'm the only one
who can find things.

– Peter, 17, Blind

Artwork by Collaborative Group, VSA Colorado/Access Gallery

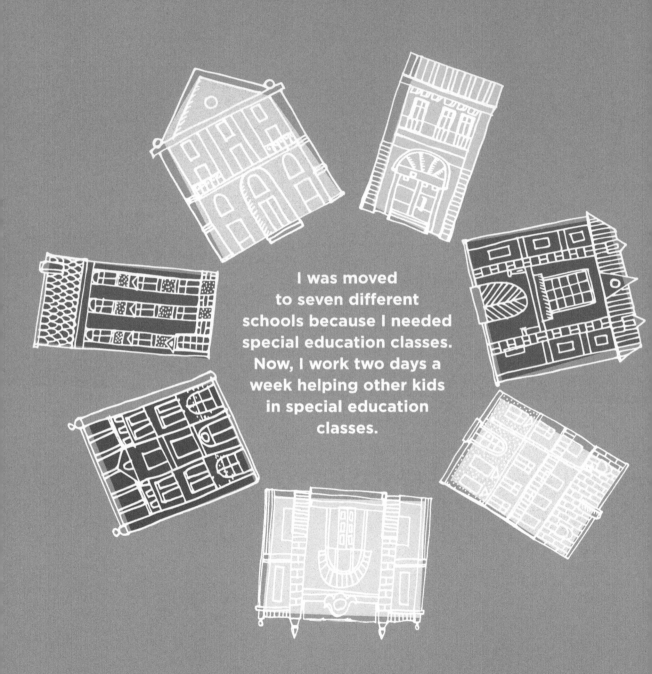

I was moved
to seven different
schools because I needed
special education classes.
Now, I work two days a
week helping other kids
in special education
classes.

– Ben, 18, Intellectual Disability

What makes me so proud about myself
is fighting through the pain.

– Jewel, 12, Congenital Heart Disease

Artwork by Shelley, 17, Friedreich's Ataxia

I like myself;
I don't want

Artwork by Collaborative Group, MDA

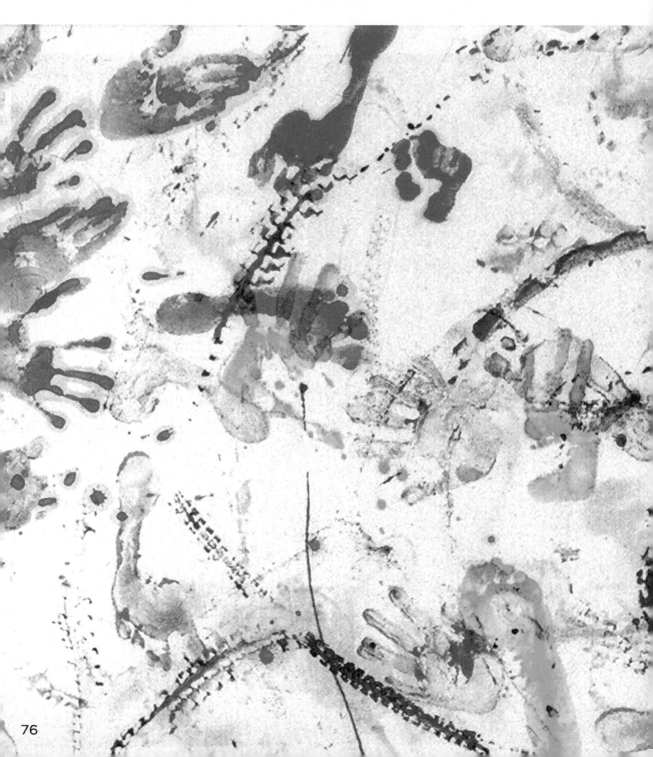

to be anyone else.

– Kyle, 11, Congenital Heart Disease

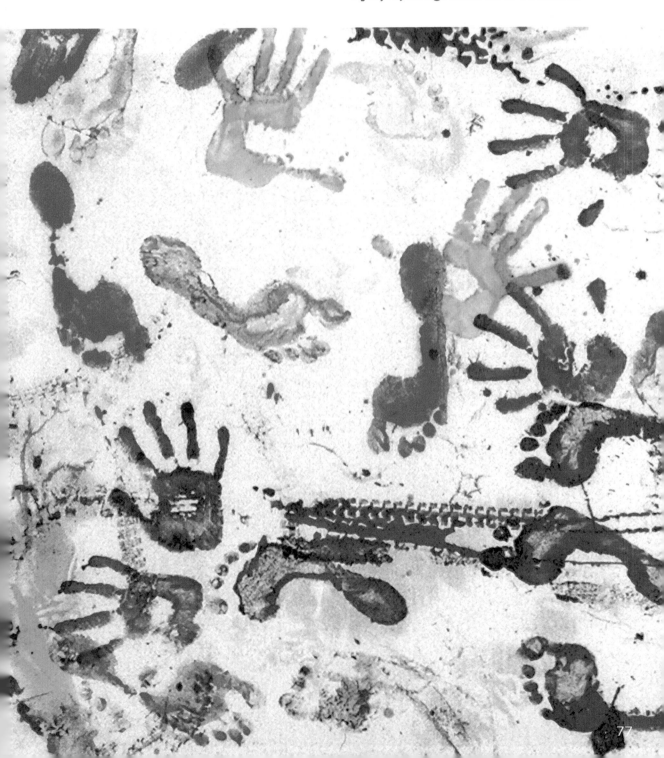

I'M REALLY PROUD THAT I WAS ABLE TO LETTER ALL FOUR YEARS FOR THE HIGH SCHOOL SWIM TEAM AND THAT I LETTERED TWO YEARS IN ACADEMICS.

– Kyle, 19, Intellectual Disability

was bullied a lot in school. People treated me differently even
though they really didn't know me.

– Hannah, 19, Intellectual Disability

Artwork by Sammy, 12, Muscular Dystrophy

I've had a girlfriend for two years.

Her name is Lizzie. She's really nice.

– Sean, 18, Intellectual Disability

Artwork by Sunia, 18, Autism

Artwork by Collaborative Group, VSA Colorado/Access Gallery

I'm proud of myself because I knew something was wrong with me. I told my grandmother and she took me to the hospital and that is when they told me I have sugar diabetes. It was scary, but I've gotten used to it.

– Blake, 13, Diabetes

I'm proud of myself because I make it through the pain.

– Rylee, 11, Dermatomyositis

I notice when people need help—and I'm always looking for ways to help them. I can't do big stuff, but I can give them pencils or cheer them on.

– Evan, 15, Muscular Dystrophy

I'm proud of myself because I got over a time of depression and a time of thoughts about suicide.

– Nick, 13, Heart Disease

Artwork by Sammy, 7, Muscular Dystrophy

When I was an Eagle Scout
I designed and built
wheelchair-accessible picnic
tables so that handicapped
people can have picnics.
It's located on a fishing dock.

– Reggie, 20, Autism

Artwork by Nicole, 17, Developmental Disability

86

IF YOU DON'T SAY, "HELLO" TO A PERSON OR ASK THEM ABOUT THEMSELVES HOW WILL YOU EVER GET TO KNOW THEM? WHO KNOWS HOW MANY AMAZING PEOPLE YOU MIGHT MISS IN LIFE IF YOU DON'T EVEN MAKE EYE CONTACT.

PEOPLE WOULD BE SURPRISED TO KNOW

I am an actual superhero. My power is being a good friend and surviving.

– Elizabeth, 16, Cancer Survivor

Artwork by Alyssa, 16, Spinal Muscular Atrophy

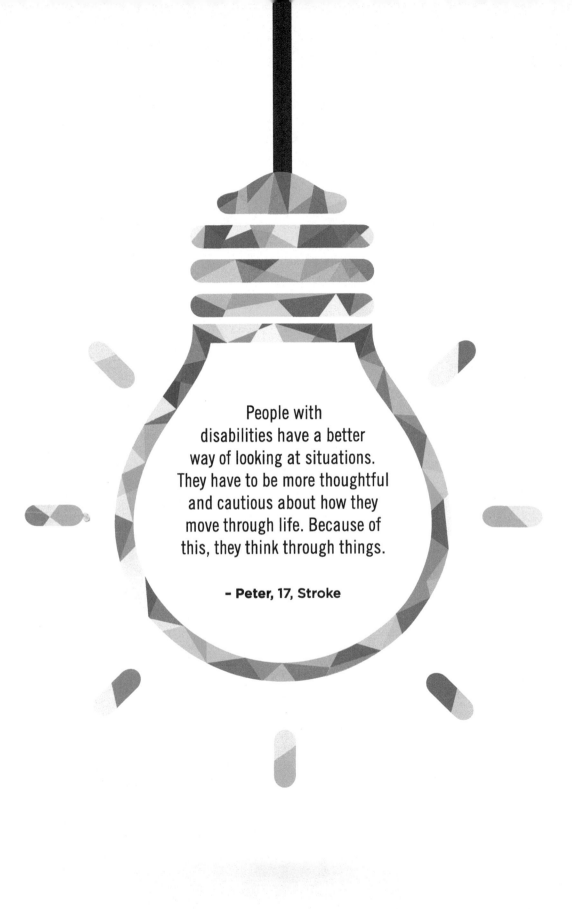

People with
disabilities have a better
way of looking at situations.
They have to be more thoughtful
and cautious about how they
move through life. Because of
this, they think through things.

– Peter, 17, Stroke

I WANT TO BE
A SINGER NAMED
IZZY SPARKS.

– Isabel, 10, Asthma

Artwork by Allie, 18, Autism

I WANT TO BE
A SINGER NAMED
IZZY SPARKS.

– Isabel, 10, Asthma

Artwork by Allie, 18, Autism

I worry a lot about
natural disasters.

– Nick, 13, Heart Disease

I

ENJOY

TAE KWON DO,

AND PLAYING THE

FLUTE AND PIANO.

– Katrina, 14, Blind

I'm VERY insecure and get
nervous around people.

– Alicia, 16, Obesity

Artwork by Jackie, 18, Autism

Artwork by Reagan, 8, Spinal Muscular Atrophy

PEOPLE THINK THOSE OF US WITH DIFFERENT CHALLENGES NEED LOTS OF HELP. BUT THE TRUTH IS, WE HAVE A LOT TO TEACH THE ABLE-BODIED.

ADVICE FOR THE ABLE-BODIED

EVERYONE HAS HARDSHIPS AT SOME TIME IN THEIR LIFE BUT OURS ARE PERMANENT AND ALWAYS AROUND. IT'S UPSETTING TO ME WHEN PEOPLE ASSOCIATE PHYSICAL DISABILITY WITH MENTAL ABILITY; I'M JUST AS SMART AS OTHER KIDS. WHEN PEOPLE STARE AT ME IT'S RUDE AND I WISH THEY WOULD JUST ASK ME WHY I WALK DIFFERENTLY.

Sarah, 16, Arthrogryposis Multiplex Congenita

I don't mind when people ask
why I'm in a chair. I wish they would.
This is a part of me.
I'm not embarrassed by it.

– **Zak**, 17, Duchenne Muscular Dystrophy

**Artwork by Luke, 13,
Spinal Muscular Atrophy**

1

Address a person with a disability directly.

2

Be patient and wait for a response.

3

Don't assume we are hard of hearing.

4

Don't touch our communication devices. Respect our space.

- Lauren, 32, Mentor for children who are speech-impaired due to autism, motor neurone disease, cerebral palsy and other disorders

Say hi.
Acknowledge us.
It's not that hard.

– Evan, 15, Muscular Dystrophy

Hello!

I WISH MORE PEOPLE WOULD START ACTING LIKE WE ARE PART OF NORMAL SOCIETY. WE ARE. WE JUST MOVE IN A DIFFERENT WAY.

– Shawn, 15, Duchenne Muscular Dystrophy

Artwork by Collaborative Group, VSA Colorado/Access Gallery

Modeled after Picasso's Guernica, this VSA collaboration led by artist Javier Flores, depicts the "no vote" by the U.S. Senate of the 2012 United Nations Convention on Rights of Persons with Disabilities. Article I States:
The purpose of the Convention is to promote, protect and ensure the full and equal enjoyment of all human rights and fundamental freedoms by all persons with disabilities, and to promote respect for their inherent dignity.

This could be you. This is us.

I'd like to ask the kids at my school to hang out with me.
Try it for one day. Come up and talk to me.

– Zak, 17, Duchenne Muscular Dystrophy

Artwork by Mariana, 7, Endocrine Myopathies

I would tell able-bodied people don't take life for granted and appreciate your ability to do things by and for yourself.

– John, 20, Muscular Dystrophy

Artwork by Nicole, 17, Developmental Disability

Don't think I can't do things for myself just because I'm blind. I don't mind if you ask if I need help, but don't try to force your help on me.

– **Peter**, 17, Blind

DON'T MAKE FUN OF PEOPLE WHO WALK FUNNY!!!

– Julie, 17, Muscular Dystrophy

I wish people would accept and understand my condition instead of assuming nothing is wrong because they can't see it on the outside.

– Cara, 13, Crohn's Disease, Ulcerative Colitis

Artwork by Allie, 18, Autism

NO MATTER WHAT YOU'RE GOING THROUGH,
WE'RE ALL IN THIS TOGETHER.
EACH OF US CAN LEARN A LITTLE SOMETHING FROM THE OTHER.

ADVICE TO KIDS WITH DISABILITIES

Have faith that your disease is not going to define
you and that you are going to come out of your
situation even stronger than when you went in.

– Bailey, 14, Congenital Heart Disease

Artwork by Darius, 18, Mental Illness

NO MATTER WHAT, KEEP ON GOING
AND WORK AT BELIEVING IN YOURSELF SO YOU
CAN BE CONFIDENT AND COMPASSIONATE.

– Hannah, 19, Intellectual Disability

LIFE IS NOT OVER WHEN YOU ARE DIAGNOSED WITH A DISABILITY.

– Corey, 19, Muscular Dystrophy

Artwork by Samuel, 10, Charcot-Marie-Tooth Disease

Artwork by Sarah, 8, Spinal Muscular Atrophy

YOU WILL GET THROUGH IT. NEVER GIVE UP. ASK FOR HELP WHEN

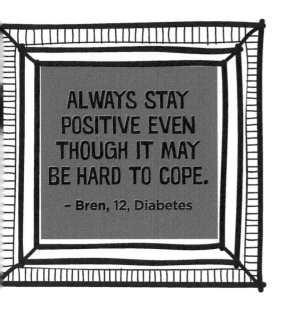

ALWAYS STAY POSITIVE EVEN THOUGH IT MAY BE HARD TO COPE.

— Bren, 12, Diabetes

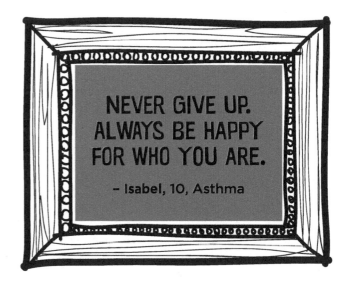

NEVER GIVE UP. ALWAYS BE HAPPY FOR WHO YOU ARE.

— Isabel, 10, Asthma

YOU'RE IN A TIGHT BUNCH.
— Greg, 13, Cyclic Vomiting

Artwork by Louis, 18, Intellectually Challenged

TAKE YOUR MEDS!

Make sure you make mature decisions that will benefit you.

– Alan, 16, Kidney Disease

My advice for other kids with medical conditions is to accept it and know you always have a network of people supporting you, so speak up when something is unusual.

– Cara, 13, Crohn's Disease, Ulcerative Colitis

BE YOURSELF.

– Rylee, 11, Dermatomyositis

Artwork by AJ, 17, Autism

Artwork by Julia, 11, Congenital Muscular Dystrophy

HOLD ONTO YOUR CHILDHOOD AND DON'T GROW UP TOO FAST.
IF YOU DO GROW UP TOO FAST, IT CAN BE NICE TO GROW BACK DOWN.

– Elizabeth, 16, PTSD, Cancer

IF WE COULD KNOW WHAT OTHER PEOPLE ARE FEELING AND THINKING AND DEALING WITH EACH DAY, DON'T YOU THINK WE'D ALL BE JUST A LITTLE MORE KIND AND FORGIVING?

WHAT'S IT LIKE?

**MY CANCER IS
A WHIRLWIND.**

– Elizabeth, 16, Cancer

122

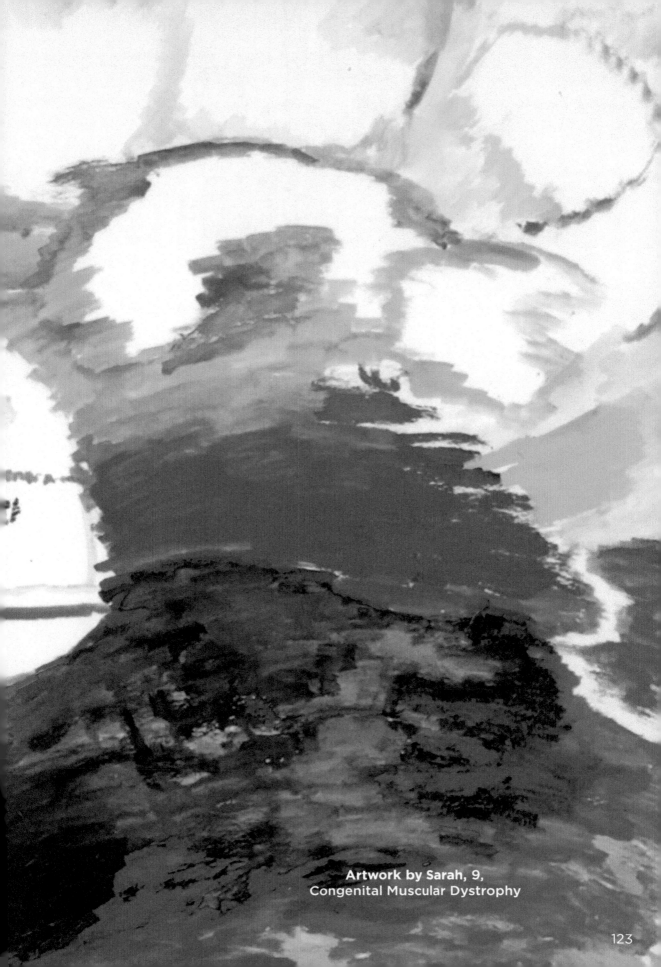

Artwork by Sarah, 9,
Congenital Muscular Dystrophy

My medical condition is gastroparesis.
This condition looks like an earthquake.
This condition sounds like a run-down car engine.
This condition smells like rotten eggs.
This condition tastes like throw-up.
This condition feels like you're getting punched in the stomach.

– Sierra, 10, Gastroparesis

My Crohn's disease is a volcano about to erupt.

– Cara, 13, Crohn's Disease

Artwork by Allie, 18, Autism

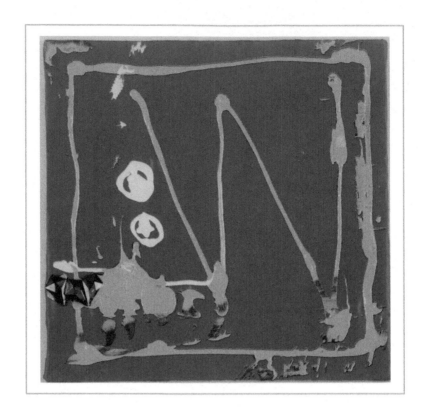

MY MUSCLES ARE LIKE TIGHT RUBBER BANDS.

– Rylee, 11, Dermatomyositis

Artwork by Nick, 9,
Becker Muscular Dystrophy

**Artwork by Timmy, 9,
Myasthenia Gravis**

My tumor feels like being
locked in a prison. I want to
move my fingers but I can't.
- Pedro, 10, Brain Tumor

MY DIABETES IS A YO-YO THAT BRINGS ME UP AND DOWN IN LIFE.

– Bren, 12, Diabetes

HELLO. IT'S ME. I'M HERE INSIDE.
THANKS FOR ASKING ME TO COME OUT
AND TELL YOU ABOUT MYSELF.
I HAVE SO MUCH TO SHARE.

WHO I AM

I WORK AT CHILDREN'S HOSPITAL.

I'm highly enjoying it. I enjoy whatever I'm doing. I like giving speeches. I like writing poems. I was in a Red Robin commercial. I've spoken at Nuggets games. I do volunteer work at my church. I've worked hard my entire life. I like everything about life. I love skiing. I love the stage. I love the spotlight. I have a huge ego. I'm kind. I'm charming. I'm everything everybody is looking for. I'm full of confidence. I'm only nervous with boys. I'm a boy magnet. I'm a babe. Michael is my boyfriend. We've been together two years. He's going to propose to me in December. I'm still deciding how I'll respond. I'm thinking of saying 'yes.' We've already planned the wedding. He is everything to me. I want to be a wellness coach, an ambassador for people with disabilities. Or maybe an actress or a choreographer. Ha! Fat chance. I'm training to be in a triathlon. It's a short one—it takes 30 minutes to do the whole thing. What I want to tell people? When life gets you down, you can get back up. Don't let other people bother you. Everything is going to be okay. Whatever you want to do, go for it—don't be afraid, get out there, take your own future in your hands. My biggest goal is to own my own limo. Oh, and to ride a horse. I hate people telling me what to do. I say yes to everything. Sometimes I don't know my own limits.

– Hannah, 19, Leukemia and Intellectually Disabled

Today, I am grief.

I am Legos.

I am green.

I am blue.

I am Harry Potter.

I am superheroes.

I am books.

I am ladybugs.

I am sobbing in
the night.

I am laughter.

I am jokes.

I am ripping paper.

I am the joker's laugh.

I am a Lego bucket
tipping back and forth.

I am hospital rooms.

I am plastic.

I am tissues.

I am tears.

I am sugar.

I am feeding
tube formula.

I am medicine.

I am a bald head.

I am sand.

I am ladybug legs tickling your hand.

I am tears dripping on your skin.

Today, I am.

– Elizabeth, 16, Cancer

DESCRIBE YOUR CONDITION

Dangerous
Intense
Annoying
Bazaar
Epic
Threatening
Everlasting
Sugar-free

– Kerri, 15, Diabetes

Problematic
Out of breath
Tiring
Slowing

**– Nick, 13, Postural Orthostatic
Tachycardia Syndrome**

Shaky
Eh
Icky
Zany
Unpredictable
Rough
Eruption
Stressful

- Patrice, 15, Seizure Disorder

Annoying
Lackluster
Preposterous
Onerous
Raging
Tiring

- Alan, 16, Alport Syndrome

WE ARE ATHLETES!

Julian

Cody

Coney with Partner Audrey

Chris

Ibsen

Gina with Partner Meg

Photos courtesy of Special Olympics Colorado/Kent Meireis

UPS AND DOWNS

Unfortunately, when I was 11 I learned I had cancer.
Fortunately, they caught it when they did.
Unfortunately, I didn't react well to chemo.
Fortunately, I met Taylor.
Unfortunately, I got a fever after every chemo.
Fortunately, the chemo was helping.
Unfortunately, I lost too much weight.
Fortunately, I finished half of chemo.
Unfortunately, I needed a surgery that lasted 11 hours.
Fortunately, it went well.
Unfortunately, I was in a lot of pain.
Fortunately, I was able to start chemo again.
Unfortunately, I got an infection.
Fortunately, I got a break from chemo.
Unfortunately I was in the hospital for three months.
Fortunately, I was released from the hospital.
Unfortunately, I had to start chemo again.
Fortunately, I finished chemo.
Unfortunately, I was having kidney problems.
Fortunately, I learned to walk again.
Unfortunately, my friend Taylor died.
Fortunately, I still got to see his mom.
Unfortunately, I got another cancer.
Fortunately, it only needed surgery.
Unfortunately, it came back.
Fortunately, there was treatment for it.
Unfortunately, it made me sick.
Fortunately, there was another treatment available.
Unfortunately, it put me in the hospital.
Fortunately, I got into a medical day care program and made friends.
Unfortunately, I was diagnosed with anxiety and PTSD.
Fortunately, both cancers are gone.

– Elizabeth, 16, Cancer

Unfortunately, when I was 10 I learned I had a heart condition.

Fortunately, the doctors could treat it.

Unfortunately, they could not cure it.

Fortunately, I can get the help I need at medical day treatment.

Unfortunately, I am almost always sick.

- Jodi, 11, Heart Condition

Unfortunately, I learned about my kidney failure at the age of four.

Fortunately, I lived a mostly normal childhood.

Unfortunately, I also had asthma.

Fortunately, my asthma is well-controlled.

Unfortunately, I started dialysis in September of last year.

Fortunately, I've been coping with dialysis for over a year and I am not on the transplant list.

- Alan, 16, Kidney Failure

Artwork by Collaborative Group,
VSA Colorado/Access Gallery

I feel proud when I get dialysis and when I get the right answer on questions.

People tell me I'm funny.

Most of the time I feel happy.

When I get scared I tell someone.

People would be surprised to learn that I like to do art.

I wish that I could be an artist when I grow up.

I wish people wouldn't think I'm sick all the time.

My medical condition is dialysis.

My favorite color is blue.

This color sounds like the ocean.

This color feels like happy.

– Sydney, 9, Kidney Disease

HEROES SELDOM WEAR CAPES.
THEY REALLY NEVER FLY. BUT THEY DO HAVE
MAGICAL POWERS THAT CHANGE EVERYONE
AROUND THEM FOR THE BETTER.

THE VIEW FROM OUTSIDE

WORKING WITH THESE KIDS IS TEACHING ME NOT TO BE UPTIGHT ABOUT THINGS THAT DON'T MATTER.

– Cassidy, 20, Easter Seals Camp Counselor

Artwork by Samuel, 9, Charcot-Marie-Tooth Disease

THESE KIDS PUSH THEMSELVES TO THEIR ABSOLUTE
DO A ZIP LINE, THEY WILL GET

LIMITS. IF THEY WANT TO CLIMB A HILL OR THERE DESPITE THEIR PHYSICAL LIMITATIONS.

– Vince, 17, Easter Seals Camp Counselor

Artwork by Ximena, 17, Leukemia

*My daughter continually inspires me.
She figures out what she needs to do and does it.
The love and pride I have for my daughter is
exactly the same as the love and pride other
parents have for their children.*

– Lynn, Daughter with Cerebral Palsy

MY BROTHER TEACHES ME
BRAVENESS.

– Tommy, 10, Brother with Hemophilia

Artwork by Kaalan, 14, Duchenne Muscular Dystrophy

WHAT HAVE I LEARNED FROM THESE KIDS?

WORKING WITH THESE

THAT IT'S NOT ALL ABOUT ME.

– Maggie, 21, Camp Counselor

KIDS IS TEACHING ME TO BE SELFLESS

AND TO FORGET ABOUT MY NEEDS FOR A LITTLE WHILE.

– Gibran, 25, Camp Counselor

Artwork by Abbey, 11, Charcot-Marie-Tooth Disease

My son never gives up. Although his speech is difficult to comprehend, he will do everything possible to help people understand what he is trying to say. He'll play charades, he'll try to think of another word, he'll spell the word, he'll give you the first letter. He does all this and never gets mad, he just keeps trying!

– **Mary Joe**, Son with Down Syndrome

People with disabilities are just normal people but with different ways of doing some things. Just like, you're a girl, I'm a boy. It's no big deal.

Chris, 10, Brother with Hemophilia

Artwork by Shawna, 6, Spinal Muscular Atrophy

APPENDIX

BULLYING IS HARMFUL

According to the National Center for Education Statistics, nearly one in three students report being bullied during the school year. On its own, this is a staggering statistic. But when you consider that children with disabilities are two to three times more likely than other students to be bullied, you begin to see how vulnerable children with physical, intellectual and medical challenges really are.

Students who experience bullying are at increased risk for depression, anxiety, sleep difficulties and poor school adjustment. Approximately 160,000 teens skip school every day because they are bullied, and one in 10 teens drops out of school due to repeated bullying.

A recent UCLA study found that bullying peaks in middle school, while children are making the transition from children to young adults.

BULLYING TARGETS

Unfortunately, children and teens who are considered "different" from their peers are the most frequent targets of bullies. These include special needs students, lesbian, gay, bisexual, and transgender students, students who are overweight and students who are perceived as "weak." Of special needs kids who report bullying, the majority of those are students with Asperger's Syndrome and students with Attention Deficit Hyperactivity Disorder.

Cyberbullying has also become prevalent between teens. About 80 percent of all high school students have encountered being bullied online in some fashion.

BEST INTERVENTION

Students who experience bullying report that peer support (i.e., spending time with the student, talking to him/her, helping him/her get away or giving advice) was the most helpful action to prevent and/or alleviate the effects of bullying. In fact, students who experience bullying find peer support much more helpful than self-action or turning to educators for assistance. Furthermore, if non-bullied students believe they can make a difference, they're more likely to intervene in a bullying situation.

ANTI–BULLYING PREVENTION PROGRAMS

Current research indicates that programs like the Sammy Loewi Buddy Program (see Appendix, page 156) can reduce bullying by helping students become better educated about disabilities, as well as more compassionate and socially sensitive.

 Through his ground-breaking research, Dr. Dan Olweus found that a school-wide approach is needed to address bullying, especially the bullying that occurs outside the classroom (e.g., in the lunchroom, hallways and schoolyard, as well as during physical education classes). His research found that if bullying behavior is ignored it becomes the norm. But when bullying is recognized and addressed, positive behavioral norms can be created and reinforced. Over time, these new norms make bullying unacceptable.

 Dr. Ron Slaby found that peer bystanders were present in 85 percent of bullying situations, and they played a key role in resolving conflicts and preventing cruelty and violence. This shows that bullying typically occurs when others are present and suggests that adolescents can learn skills to solve problems in nonviolent ways.

 According to Tom Tarshis, director of the Bay Area Children's Association, positive peer pressure is an important component of effective intervention. "When uninvolved students step up and let the perpetrator know that their behavior is not acceptable, it sends a powerful message," Tarshis explains.

A three-year study of anti-bullying programs promoted by the Colorado Trust Foundation found that when bullying is low and a school's climate/culture is considered high, overall academic achievement is much higher than at schools where bullying is more prevalent. In fact, in schools that ranked the highest on positive school climate (and thus, low on bullying), 78 percent of students scored at proficient or advanced in math versus only 34 percent of students in schools with a less positive school climate.

Researchers involved with the study recommend that school administrators make bullying prevention an integral and permanent component of the school environment. More specifically, they recommend that anti-bullying themes, messages and rituals be incorporated into school curriculum and activities, and that teachers, with the support of administrators, set aside 20 to 30 minutes each week to discuss bullying and peer relations with students.

The foundation's publication, *SHOUT,* can be used as a powerful catalyst for discussion about how students are not all that different from one another. As the book makes clear, we may not look, walk, talk or act alike, but all of us share similar hopes, dreams, feelings, desires, talents and passions. We are all, in short, human beings that deserve respect.

Artwork by Student Campaign at Graland

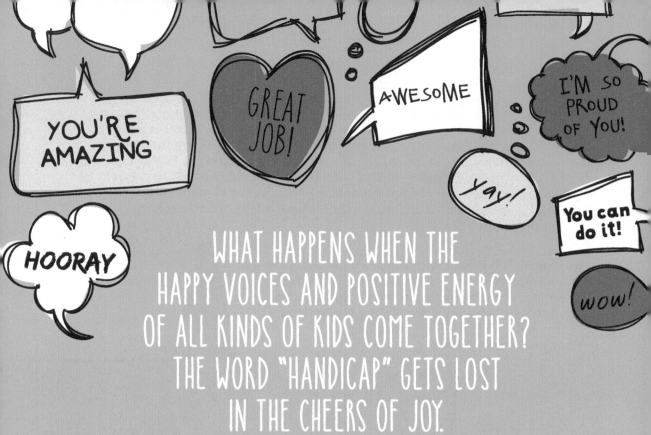

WHAT HAPPENS WHEN THE HAPPY VOICES AND POSITIVE ENERGY OF ALL KINDS OF KIDS COME TOGETHER? THE WORD "HANDICAP" GETS LOST IN THE CHEERS OF JOY.

Sammy created a legacy event at her elementary school. Here's the story and simple guidelines to create the same magic at your school.

The Graland Sammy Loewi Unified Neighborhood Games Program

When Sammy was in the fourth grade, her class at Graland Country Day School in Denver was searching for a community project. At the time, I was CEO of Special Olympics of Colorado and Sammy suggested creating a Special Olympics Day.

Her teachers loved the idea and we worked together to create an event that would pair fourth-grade students from Graland with kids from nearby special education classes to compete in four events—a basketball throw, relay race, bean bag toss and long jump. All of Sammy's classmates were shy at first, not sure how to approach kids they considered to be "different." But once the children started playing together, all perceived differences disappeared and they began to laugh and play together easily.

"BEFORE THAT EXPERIENCE, I WOULD LOOK AT DISABLED PEOPLE AND TRY TO KEEP AS FAR AWAY FROM THEM AS POSSIBLE. I WAS HONESTLY SUPER SCARED AND NERVOUS. BUT WHEN I GOT OFF THE BUS AND SAW 11 SMILING FACES I KNEW IT MEANT A LOT TO THEM. WHEN I MET MY BUDDY HE INSTANTLY TALKED AND HE WAS THE NICEST KID EVER AND COMPLETELY NORMAL. AFTER OUR FIRST FEW MEETINGS I KNEW HIM WELL AND I KNEW IT MEANT A LOT TO ME."

– Linc, Graland student

That simple one-day program 15 years ago has since evolved into an ongoing year-long program that partners Graland students with children with special needs. Now known as the Graland Sammy Loewi Unified Neighborhood Games, the program pairs students based on interest and temperament. Those pairs come together regularly over the course of the school year for a variety of activities. They begin with simple get-acquainted meetings and evolve to bowling outings, holiday get-togethers, joint art projects and picnics, and finally, a Special Olympics competition at the end of the school year.

"The buddy program is an amazing experience and I wish everyone could do it. It's unbelievable!"
– Sloan

In addition to becoming friends with special education students, Graland students create and manage a school-wide campaign to stop bullying against students with disabilities. Their goal: to teach classmates never to use the "R word" when describing someone with physical and/or intellectual challenges. Graland students also share what they've learned about children with disabilities at a school-wide assembly.

"If I hadn't met my buddy, I would have turned kids with disabilities down and wouldn't have known how fun they are."
– Douglas

Fifteen years later, Graland has developed a year-long program that includes a curriculum that evaluates each month's activities.

TO SET UP THE PROGRAM AND FIND "BUDDIES" THAT ARE A PERFECT

1 Graland students are paired with nearby neighborhood special education students. The Graland students are surveyed about where they feel they can be most helpful. (Also see year-long curriculum on Page 161.)

2 The special education teachers send a detailed description to Graland of each special needs child and their challenges so the matching can be as successful as possible.

Then, a year of activities takes place, from helping guide the buddies through getting to know each other, to more interactive activities as the year goes on.

To set up a program at your school, here are suggestions for each month:

October: Get-to-know-you meetings—each fourth-grade class meets with their Unified Neighborhood (UN) school to get acquainted with their buddies.

November: Bowling—everyone meets at the bowling lanes, bowls and has lunch together.

December/January: Holiday-get-together—each fourth-grade class gets together with their buddy school for a holiday celebration (some great ginger bread houses can be made here).

January: Fourth graders present to the lower school at an assembly, sharing their thoughts and experiences with the program so far, and helping to inspire kids for the years ahead.

February: Portrait exchange. Each student draws an 8x10 portrait of their buddy. Put the portraits on display at the school and hold an art exhibit. Invite buddies to come to an ice cream party/exhibit.

March: Have the students run a school-wide campaign regarding never using the "R word" to describe someone with physical and intellectual challenges. Have students make posters in art class and write copy delivered over the school PA system.
(see page 155)

EQUAL, A POEM

Some people are mean, some are nice, some are filled with laughter and some cry, some are black, some are white, some like baseball and others like rugby, some like music and some like drama, some drink Coke and some drink Pepsi, none of all can make us different none of all can put one down, some judge a book by its cover and some read the actual inside, some take the right path and some take the left, if people choose to judge a book by its cover they can learn, people can change, we all can change and learn we are all equal, no one can make us different from each other. – Jeb, 10, Buddy Program Participant

April: At Graland, this is when the Unified Teams come together for the Special Olympics ceremony and games. The Graland fourth graders invite their parents, grandparents and older students to come to the gym and enjoy the opening ceremonies. The students write the remarks and run the entire program, introducing the current CEO from Special Olympics and a guest speaker who is intellectually challenged. Students' songs and poems are performed and there is a mock "lighting of the torch" to begin the games. At Graland, there are now up to 500 spectators in attendance watching children stand with their buddies, holding hands and singing "We Are The World." There is not a dry eye in the audience.

Kids then head outside and partner with their buddies to engage in friendly and affirming competition. The day is capped off by sharing pizza and kite-flying.

May: Spring picnics help top off the year and give buddies one last time to meet and have fun together before summer vacation.

The Graland Sammy Loewi Buddy Program can be replicated at any and every K-12 school across the country. All it takes is permission from your school administration, and identifying one or several teachers willing to work with the Special Education teacher or teachers in designing a program that can work with your specific school.

The rewards for everyone are enormous: learning that all children are valuable, that civility, kindness and compassion matter and that exclusion and bullying are never acceptable.

To find out more about Special Olympics, visit **www.specialolympicsco.org**.

SEPTEMBER MATCHING BUDDY SURVEY

The participating teachers meet with the Special Education teachers and use this survey to carefully match all of the buddies. This should be a thoughtful process to ensure a successful relationship for everyone.

NAME: _____

Think about the type of person you are. How can you be helpful? What strengths do you have that you can share with your buddy?

Read the characteristics and challenges below

• CIRCLE **THREE** that you think you could be helpful for.

• **CROSS OUT** any characteristics that you think might be too much for you to handle as a buddy.

talkative	energetic	speaks Spanish
bossy	very small	needs a patience buddy
has trouble following directions	dramatic	Autistic
very quiet	hard to understand	has tiny seizures
independent	very helpful	loud screeches
likes to wander away from the group	makes up stories	

GRALAND CURRICULUM
SAMMY LOEWI BUDDY PROGRAM

Sep.	Planning Implementation Evaluation	Meaningful Service Link to Curriculum Reflection Diversity Youth Voice Partnerships Progress Monitoring Duration and Intensity				
Oct.	Planning Implementation Evaluation	Meaningful Service Link to Curriculum Reflection Diversity Youth Voice Partnerships Progress Monitoring Duration and Intensity	Individual class discussions on special needs Reflections on first meeting Journeys: Descriptive paragraphs	Meet buddies in small settings		Bus if meeting is off campus
Nov.	Planning Implementation Evaluation	Meaningful Service Link to Curriculum Reflection Diversity Youth Voice Partnerships Progress Monitoring Duration and Intensity	Journal writing about bowling experience	Whole grade bowling and lunch with buddies		Organize with Monaco lanes Reserve buses

GRALAND CURRICULUM
SAMMY LOEWI BUDDY PROGRAM

Dec.	Planning Implementation Evaluation	Meaningful Service Link to Curriculum Reflection Diversity Youth Voice Partnerships Progress Monitoring Duration and Intensity	Lower School assembly presentation	Holiday buddy gathering and activities Group reflection and goal setting		Assembly: PowerPoint projector
Jan.	Planning Implementation Evaluation	Meaningful Service Link to Curriculum Reflection Diversity Youth Voice Partnerships Progress Monitoring Duration and Intensity	Begin reading *SHOUT* Reflective posts on class and individual blogs			Student copies of *SHOUT* Study guides, class and individual webpages
Feb.	Planning Implementation Evaluation	Meaningful Service Link to Curriculum Reflection Diversity Youth Voice Partnerships Progress Monitoring Duration and Intensity		Buddy activities	UN Art Exhibit (coordinated by Art teacher)	Art materials brought to UN Schools

Mar.	Planning Implementation Evaluation	Meaningful Service Link to Curriculum Reflection Diversity Youth Voice Partnerships Progress Monitoring Duration and Intensity	R-Word Campaign	Sportsmanship talks (PE)	Order R-word materials from Project Unity Set up Graland classroom visits	Assembly: PowerPoint projector
Apr.	Planning Implementation Evaluation	Meaningful Service Link to Curriculum Reflection Diversity Youth Voice Partnerships Progress Monitoring Duration and Intensity	Sammy Leowi Unified Neighborhood Games		PE partnership and participation	Speakers
May	Planning Implementation Evaluation	Meaningful Service Link to Curriculum Reflection Diversity Youth Voice Partnerships Progress Monitoring Duration and Intensity	Final reflections— written and oral		End-of-year get-together	

"THIS PROGRAM AFFECTED ME BY MAKING ME A BETTER PERSON AND REALIZING THAT WE ARE ALL DIFFERENT BUT REALLY ALL THE SAME." –Jack

INTERACTING WITH PEOPLE WITH DISABILITIES*

Don't make assumptions about people or their disabilities. Don't assume you know what someone wants, what he feels, or what is best for him. If you have a question about what to do, how to do it, what language or terminology to use, or what assistance to offer, ask him. That person should be your first and best resource.

Remember that people with disabilities are individuals with unique preferences. Just because one person with a disability prefers something one way doesn't mean that another person with the same disability also prefers it that way.

Ask before you help. In some cases, a person with a disability might seem to be struggling, yet she is fine and would prefer to complete the task on her own. Follow the person's cues and ask if you are not sure what to do. Don't be offended if someone declines your offer of assistance.

Talk directly to the person with disabilities, not to their interpreter, attendant or friend. You don't need to ignore the others, just make sure to focus your interaction on the person with disabilities.

> If you will be speaking for some time with a person in a wheelchair, get down so that you are at eye level with her so she doesn't have to strain her neck to look up at you.

> Speak normally. Some people have a tendency to talk louder and slower to people with disabilities; don't. Don't assume that because a person has one disability, that he also has a cognitive disability or is hard of hearing. For example, a person with cerebral palsy might use a wheelchair, have uncontrolled upper body movements, have difficulty speaking, and yet have very good hearing, cognitive abilities and intelligence.

> Use normal language including "see" and "look." It's fine to use common phrases such as, "Do you see what I mean?" even to people who are blind.

Use "people-first" language when referring to people with disabilities. People-first language means put the person first and the disability second. For example, say "a man who is blind" rather than "a blind man," and "a woman who uses a wheelchair" instead of "a wheelchair-bound woman." *(See People First Language in this Appendix.)*

Be aware of personal space. Some people who use a mobility aid, such as a wheelchair, walker or cane, see these aids as part of their personal space. Don't touch, move or lean on mobility aids. This is also important for safety.

*Copyright Shawn Lawton Henry, 2007.

PEOPLE FIRST LANGUAGE

Words are powerful. Old, inaccurate descriptors and the inappropriate use of medical diagnoses perpetuate negative stereotypes and reinforce a significant and an incredibly powerful attitudinal barrier. And this invisible, but potent, force—not the diagnosis itself—is the greatest obstacle facing individuals who have conditions we call disabilities.

When we see the diagnosis as the most important characteristic of a person, we devalue her as an individual. Do **you** want to be known for your psoriasis, gynecological history, the warts on your behind or any other condition?

Unfortunately, disability diagnoses are often used to define a person's value and potential, and low expectations and a dismal future may be the predicted norm. A person's diagnosis is often used to decide how/where the person will be educated, what type of job he will/won't have, where/how he'll live, and more, including what services he is thought to need.

If people with disabilities are to be included in all aspects of society, and if they're to be respected and valued as our fellow citizens, we must stop using language that devalues and sets them apart. Here are some examples of the many ways language can be altered to put the **person** before the disability.

Say:	Instead of:
People with disabilities.	The handicapped or disabled.
Paul has a cognitive disability (diagnosis)	He's mentally retarded.
Kate has autism (or a diagnosis of)	She's autistic.
Ryan has down syndrome (or a diagnosis of)	He's down's; a down's person; mongoloid.
Sara has a learning disability (diagnosis)	She's learning disabled.
Bob has a physical disability (diagnosis).	He's quadriplegic/is crippled.
Mary is of short stature./Mary's a little person.	She's a dwarf/midget.
Tom has a mental health condition.	He's emotionally disturbed/ mentally ill.
Nora uses a wheelchair/mobility chair.	She's confined to/is wheelchair-bound.
Steve receives special ed services.	He's in special ed; is a sped student/inclusion student.
Tonya has a developmental delay.	She's developmentally delayed.
Children without disabilities	Normal/healthy/typical kids.
Communicates with her eyes/device/etc.	Is non-verbal.
Customer	Client, consumer, recipient, etc.
Congenital disability	Birth defect.
Brain injury	Brain damaged.
Accessible parking, hotel room, etc.	Handicapped parking, hotel room, etc.
She needs or she uses	She has a problem with.../ She has special needs.

(Adapted from "People First Language" copyright 2015, Kathie Snow, www.disabilityisnatural.com; used with permission of the author).

DISABILITY AND DISEASE GLOSSARY

The children we interviewed for this book had the following diseases, disabilities and disorders:

Arthrogryposis Multiplex Congenita— Children born with this rare condition have joint contractures that cause muscle shortening and weakness. Almost every joint in the body is affected, which means overall body movement can be severely compromised. The most common type of Arthrogryposis (called Amyoplasia) affects the hands, wrists, elbows, shoulders, hips, feet and knees. In more severe types, every joint can be affected, including the jaw and spine. This is a rare disorder that occurs in one out of every 10,000 live births.

Asthma—This chronic inflammatory disease of the airways is one of the most common chronic childhood disorders—in fact, it is the third leading cause of hospitalization in children under age 15. Common symptoms include wheezing, coughing, chest tightness and shortness of breath.

Autism or Autism Spectrum Disorder— These are the general terms for a group of complex disorders of brain development. These disorders are characterized, in varying degrees, by difficulties in social interaction, verbal and nonverbal communication and repetitive behaviors. Autism can also be associated with intellectual disability, difficulties in motor coordination and attention and physical health issues such as sleep and gastrointestinal disturbances. Some persons with ASD excel in visual skills, music, math and art. About one in 68 children are affected by autism—a ten-fold increase in the last 40 years.

Cancer—Cancer, an out-of-control growth of abnormal cells, is the second leading cause of death in children (behind accidents). Leukemia and brain/central nervous system cancers are the most common childhood cancers.

Cerebral Palsy—This is a broad term used to describe a group of chronic "palsies" or disorders that impair control of movement due to damage in the developing brain. Between 35 and 50 percent of all children with CP will have an accompanying seizure disorder and some level of mental retardation. They may also have learning disabilities and vision, speech, hearing or language problems. About 10,000 infants are diagnosed with CP and up to 1,500 preschoolers in the U.S. are recognized as having it each year.

Congenital Heart Disease—This is a category of heart disease that includes abnormalities in the structure of the heart that occur before birth. These defects, which range from mild to serious, can affect a child's breathing, blood flow, ability to exercise and overall stamina. In the most serious cases, heart transplant may be required. CHD affects approximately 1 in 100 children.

Crohn's Disease—This chronic condition involves inflammation in the wall of the digestive tract. Symptoms range from mild (pain, loose stools or gassy belly), to severe, wherein a child doubles over with pain, loses weight, passes stools more than eight times a day, and passes blood. About 20 percent of all people with Crohn's disease are children.

Cyclic Vomiting—Cyclic vomiting syndrome (CVS) is a condition in which a child has repeated episodes of severe nausea and vomiting. In between these cycles, the child is generally healthy. During a CVS cycle, the child will often vomit several times per hour; the cycle can last from a few hours to a few days. Most children with CVS suffer from migraine headaches and miss a great deal of school. The cause is unknown and there is no treatment. CVS is estimated to affect up to three out of every 100,000 children in the U.S.

Dermatomyositis—This rare autoimmune disease causes skin rash, muscle weakness, stiff and swollen joints, contractures and ulcers. Children with this disease often suffer from poor appetite, weight loss and a severely compromised ability to exercise. There is no known cure. It is a rare disease that affects approximately three in every one million children.

Diabetes—This disease, in which the body's ability to process glucose is severely compromised, affects 13,000 children in the U.S. each year. Diabetes, in the short-term, can affect a child's energy and ability to gain weight. The disease can also cause long-term complications, including heart disease, stroke, vision impairment and kidney damage.

Gastroparesis—Also called delayed gastric emptying, Gastroparesis is a disorder that slows or stops the movement of food from the stomach to the small intestine. Normally, the muscles of the stomach contract to break up food and move it through the gastrointestinal GI tract. Gastroparesis occurs when the stomach muscles stop working normally.

Hemophilia—Hemophilia is a rare genetic bleeding disorder that prevents the blood from clotting properly, so a person with hemophilia bleeds more than someone without hemophilia. For kids, this means that normal childhood bumps and scrapes are a cause of extra concern. Currently, about 17,000 people in the United States have hemophilia. Hemophilia affects mostly boys—about one in every 5,000 to 10,000 is born with it. It is a life-long condition with no known cure.

Intellectual Disability—This catch-all term is used to describe a person with certain limitations in cognitive functioning and other skills, including communication and self-care. These limitations can cause a child to develop and learn more slowly or differently. Examples of intellectual disabilities include Fragile X Syndrome, Down Syndrome, Autism and Fetal Alcohol Syndrome. An estimated seven to eight million Americans have an intellectual disability, which means about one in ten families in the United States are affected by it.

Kidney Disease—Kidney disease can affect children in various ways, ranging from treatable disorders without long-term consequences to life-threatening conditions. Children with chronic kidney disease may grow at a slower rate than their peers, and urinary incontinence—the loss of bladder control, which results in the accidental loss of urine—is common. Kids with kidney disease face many challenges, which can include negative self-image, relationship problems, behavior problems, learning problems, trouble concentrating, and delayed language and/or motor skills development.

Muscular Dystrophy—Muscular dystrophy is a group of diseases that cause progressive weakness and loss of muscle mass. In muscular dystrophy, abnormal genes interfere with the production of proteins needed to form healthy muscle. There are many different kinds of muscular dystrophy, including Duchenne MD, which causes muscle degeneration and eventual death (typically by age 25). Symptoms of the most common varieties begin in childhood, primarily in boys. Some people who have muscular dystrophy will eventually lose the ability to walk. Some may have trouble breathing or swallowing. There is no cure, but medications and therapy can help manage symptoms and slow the course of the disease.

Obesity—Childhood obesity is the result of a caloric imbalance—too few calories expended for the amount of calories consumed—and is caused by various genetic, behavioral and environmental factors. The percentage of children who are overweight or obese has more than doubled in the last 20 years. Today, more than a third of children are overweight or obese. Obese youth are more likely to have risk factors for cardiovascular disease, prediabetes, bone and joint problems, such as sleep apnea, and social and psychological problems, such as stigmatization and poor self-esteem.

Seizure Disorders—also known as epilepsy—are caused by abnormal brain function. Symptoms vary between individuals, but can include loss of consciousness, repeated jerking of a single limb, generalized convulsions with uncontrollable jerking of muscles throughout the body, hand rubbing, and misplaced perceptions of an odor, sound or taste. About 200,000 people are diagnosed with epilepsy every year, 30 percent of them children. There is no cure, but various treatments can help keep symptoms under control.

Stroke—A stroke occurs when the flow of oxygen-rich blood to a portion of the brain is blocked. Without oxygen, brain cells start to die after a few minutes and cause symptoms such as sudden weakness, paralysis or numbness of the face, arms, or legs, trouble speaking or understanding speech, and trouble seeing. Strokes can affect anyone at any time, including children. In fact, stroke is one of the top ten causes of death in children.

Ulcerative Colitis—This is a chronic disease of the large intestine, also known as the colon, in which the lining of the colon becomes inflamed and develops tiny open sores, or ulcers, that produce pus and mucous. The combination of inflammation and ulceration can cause abdominal discomfort and frequent emptying of the colon. In the United States, two of every 100,000 children are affected, and 20 to 25 percent of all cases occur in persons aged 20 years or younger.

WITH SINCERE THANKS...

This book would not have been possible if the following organizations had not fully supported our project and generously allowed us to interview children who participate in their programs.

MUSCULAR DYSTROPHY ASSOCIATION OF COLORADO

The Muscular Dystrophy Association is the world's leading nonprofit health agency dedicated to finding treatments and cures for muscular dystrophy, amyotrophic lateral sclerosis (ALS), and other neuromuscular diseases. The Muscular Dystrophy Association funds worldwide research for 40 different kinds of neuromuscular diseases and provides comprehensive health care services and support to MDA families nationwide. Go to **www.mda.org** for more information.

EASTER SEALS OF COLORADO

Easter Seals has been helping individuals with disabilities and special needs, as well as their families, for nearly 100 years. The organization's long list of support services includes child development centers, physical rehabilitation and job training services. To find out more go to **www.eastersealscolorado.org.**

The Rocky Mountain Village in Empire, Colorado, one of the top Easter Seals camps in the country, was instrumental in helping this book come to fruition. The camp is fully accessible and used by more than 800 children and adults with disabilities every year. Here, campers enjoy swimming, fishing, overnight camping, outdoor cooking, day trips, arts and crafts, sports and recreation, hiking, dances, music and drama, horseback riding, and riding the zipline.

SPECIAL OLYMPICS COLORADO

Founded in 1969, the mission of SOCO is to provide year-round sports training and athletic competition in a variety of Olympic-type sports for children and adults with intellectual disabilities. The sports program gives participants continuing opportunities to develop physical fitness, demonstrate courage, experience joy and share their gifts, skills and friendship with their families, other Special Olympics athletes and the community. For more information, go to **www.specialolympicsco.org.**

SOCO PROJECT UNIFY (PROGRAM OF SPECIAL OLYMPICS COLORADO)

This school-based program uses sports and leadership programs to motivate young people to develop school communities where all youth can become agents of change. Project Unify is designed to foster respect, dignity and advocacy for people with intellectual disabilities. To learn more, contact the Project UNIFY Youth Initiatives Manager at 720-359-3117.

GLOBAL DOWN SYNDROME FOUNDATION

Global Down Syndrome Foundation is a public nonprofit dedicated to significantly improving the lives of people with Down syndrome through Research, Medical Care, Education and Advocacy. Global supports two affiliates which together constitute the only academic home in the United States committed solely to research and medical care for people with Down syndrome - the Crnic Institute for Down Syndrome and the Sie Center for Down Syndrome. To learn more, visit **www.globaldownsyndrome.org**.

COLORADO CENTER FOR THE BLIND, LITTLETON, COLORADO

The Colorado Center for The Blind helps people with blindness gain the self-confidence necessary to gain independence, pursue opportunities and achieve success. The center offers many unique learning activities, such as inviting students with visual impairment to dissect small sharks. Blind students leave the Colorado Center training program as living examples of the motto: "With effective training and opportunity, blind people can compete on terms of equality with their sighted peers." To learn more, contact the Center at **ccb@cocenter.org.**

CHILDREN'S HOSPITAL OF COLORADO (MEDICAL DAY TREATMENT PROGRAM)

Established in 1991, Medical Day Treatment is a collaborative venture between Children's Hospital Colorado and Aurora Public Schools. The program's mission is to improve the quality of life for children and adolescents with chronic medical illnesses who face barriers to accessing education. Medical Day Treatment nurses, teachers, and mental health staff work as a team collaboratively with the youth and their families to empower them to reach academic goals, improve medical adherence and stability, and optimize emotional well-being. For more information, call 720-777-6200.

2HEARTS

2HEARTS aims to ensure that all teens with Congenital Heart Disease have the resources needed to lead stable, healthy lives. 2HEARTS provides a support network for children with Congenital Heart Disease. They get to meet others who have experienced similar pains and fears. They have a network of other kids who have scars, pacemakers and daily medicines, as well as other kids who understand what it feels like to spend weeks in a hospital, to not be able to participate in P.E., or to wait years on the heart transplant list. Visit **www.2-hearts.org.**

The majority of art you see in this book came from the following three organizations, all of which overwhelmed us with their extreme generosity and enthusiastic help with this project.

MDA ART COLLECTION

The Muscular Dystrophy Association Art Collection was established in 1992 to focus attention on the achievements of artists with disabilities and to emphasize that physical disability is no barrier to creativity. The Collection, on display at MDA's national office in Chicago, Illinois, and the operations center in Tucson, Arizona, comprises 400 original works by adults and children who have any of the neuromuscular disorders in MDA's program. Artists in the Collection represent all 50 states, the District of Columbia and Puerto Rico, and ranged in age from 2 to 84 when the artwork was created. The variety of talented young people living with neuromuscular diseases is astounding. Their art speaks volumes about their courage, hopes and dreams. To view more of their art go to **www.mda.org.**

VSA COLORADO/ACCESS GALLERY

Founded in 1978 in Colorado, VSA Colorado/Access Gallery is an inclusive, international, nonprofit organization offering creative and educational opportunities for people with disabilities to access and experience the arts. Much of the art you see in this book was discovered at the VSA Colorado/ Access Gallery. Each year, VSA Colorado/Access Gallery serves nearly 10,000 people with disabilities, their families and those who work with them. Their studio is located at 909 Santa Fe Drive, Denver, CO 80204. For more information go to **www.accessgallery.org.**

ROUNDUP RIVER RANCH

Roundup River Ranch provides free, year-round programs and camp experiences to all children with serious illnesses and their families in the Rocky Mountain region. Campers share in the true joys of old-fashioned camp fun and making new friends, while their parents have peace of mind that the camp is staffed with trained volunteers and medical professionals. Campers have provided several of the art pieces that you see in the book. For more information on this unique camp go to **www.roundupriverranch.org.**

ACKNOWLEDGMENTS

To say that *SHOUT* has been a collaborative project is an understatement. From the 90 courageous youth that were willing to be interviewed to the many talented artists who are showcased in the book, I give my undying gratitude. To my children, who inspired this book more than they will ever know—Kimberly Ann, Samantha Michelle, Jeffrey John—and to Sammy's dear father, Andy, I am forever grateful for your examples, love and support.

To my friend, writing coach and co-conspirator Shari Caudron, thank you for asking the right questions at the right time and inspiring me and assisting me throughout this writing journey. To Cheryl Patrick, whose design sensibility and creative panache can be felt throughout the entire book, you have been nothing short of a pleasure with whom to work. To my dear friend and terrific editor Kristi Fisher, thank you for your continued support and the boundless energy you pour into whatever project you undertake. Your creative perspective and endless talent never cease to amaze me. And to my dear friend Ann Kiley, whose friendship and initial legal counsel allowed and inspired me to continue with this project.

An enormous thank you to my dear friend Cole Finegan and his A-plus legal team at Hogan Lovells: Matt, Kathleen, Nicole and Jared, who charted me through challenging legal waters and made the navigating much more manageable. And to my tax pals at Crowe GHP Horwath, Angie Kennedy and team, I can't begin to thank you enough.

Also thank you to my friends at the Muscular Dystrophy Association: Sabrina Allen and Joanne Shortt; Special Olympics of Colorado: Mindy Watrous; Easter Seals of Colorado: Lynn Robinson; VSA Colorado: Damon McLease and Cris Ciani; and teachers Kerra Zambrano and Teresa Johnson at Children's Hospital of Colorado Medical Day Treatment Program. Without your encouragement and complete support this book could not have happened.

My continued admiration for all the parents, teachers and caregivers who devote so much of their precious time and energy to making life richer for children who are physically, medically and intellectually challenged. To all of Sammy's caregivers, our family is forever grateful for your loving care.

To my family, Steve, Darla, Sue, Bob and Kathy, thank you for always being there when most needed. To my parents, Mae and Theron, who taught me to embrace difference, for that I am forever grateful.

And last but not least, thank you to Sammy's loyal Graland friends, Sam, Alana, Sarah, Peter and Martha for being such a network of support and love. And, to her dear friends Amber Hecht and Monterey Buchanan, for facing each day with enormous courage, talent and determination that continues to inspire us all.

Pat Loewi

WE SHOULD ALL TREAT EACH OTHER
MORE LIKE DOGS TREAT US.

THEY ARE ALWAYS HAPPY TO SEE US.
THEY DON'T JUDGE.

THEY KISS YOU EVEN IF YOU HAVE BAD BREATH.

THEY ARE NEVER BOSSY AND ALWAYS LOYAL.

THEY SEE THE REAL YOU INSIDE.

THEY NEVER EVEN NOTICE A DISABILITY,
UNLESS IT'S TO NOTICE YOU COULD USE
A HELPING PAW

SAMMY AND ANNIE
LOVE AT FIRST LICK

ABOUT THE AUTHOR

Patricia Fotheringham Loewi was born and raised in Salt Lake City, Utah, where she taught English and history before moving to Washington, D.C. Pat worked on Capitol Hill doing press work in those halcyon days when Congress was collaborating.

She is currently living in Denver, Colorado, near her daughter Kim, Kim's husband Jeff, and her three granddaughters. (Pat's husband, Andy, passed away from kidney cancer in 2007). Pat has spent most of her professional career in telecommunications, radio ownership and nonprofit work. She served as CEO for Special Olympics Colorado as well as the Kempe Foundation for Abused and Neglected Children. However, she admits to learning most about kids who are "different" from her daughter Sammy's experiences of feeling marginalized. Sammy was in a wheelchair with Ullrich Congenital Muscular Dystrophy from the age of 10 until her untimely death at age 22.

Pat is therefore motivated to help change the culture by promoting kindness, compassion and acceptance of kids who are "different."

CPSIA information can be obtained
at www.ICGtesting.com
Printed in the USA
LVOW05s2047040116
469052LV00040B/266/P